How To Build A Website

(Master Key Elements To Set Yourself Up For Success)

The Beginner's Guide To Building Your Most Important Digital Asset - Your Website!

ARX Reads

Copyright © 2020 ARX Reads LLC

All rights reserved.

No part of this publication may be reproduced, stored in a retrieval system, or transmitted, in any form or by any means, electronic, photocopying, recording or otherwise, without the prior written permission of the publisher, or as expressly permitted by law, or under terms agreed with the appropriate reprographic rights organization.

Inquiries concerning reproduction outside the scope of the above should be sent to the Rights Department at the address below. You must not circulate this book in any other binding or cover and you must impose this same condition on any acquirer.

ARX Reads LLC

info@arxreads.com

www.arxreads.com

Table of Contents

WHY YOU NEED A WEBSITE 4

HOW TO SET UP A WEBSITE 8

5 ALTERNATIVE WAYS TO BUILD A WEBSITE 12

TOOLS FOR WEBSITES 15

KEYS TO A GREAT WEBSITE 19

DRIVING TRAFFIC TO YOUR WEBSITE 24

STATS FOR SUCCESS 28

A GIVEAWAY 32

Why You Need A Website

Creating an online business will take time and effort. The best tool for reaching others is by having a website. This chapter provides the numerous advantages a website can offer.

Reasons Having A Website Can Help Any Business

Reason #1: **Your Online Home.**

- Where people can go to find what you offer.
- A specific place that allows others to locate the necessary products and services with ease.

Reason #2: **Credibility.**

CREDIBILITY

- Individuals will put greater confidence in what is being sold.
- Higher likelihood of getting and keeping customers or clients by having a website.

Reason #3: **Control.**

- Having a professional website means more control.
- Critical if you're a business owner to have total control.

Reason #4: **Different Needs For Different Businesses.**

Different Needs For Different Businesses

- It's possible to create pages for various company goals.
- Make an opt-in page for any type of business to get individuals on an email list.
- Create product pages that show what is being offered.

Reason #5: **Free Content—Digital Publishing.**

- Offering valuable information to an audience by blogging.
- Solving problems and creating solutions while answering questions.

Reason #6: **Highlighting Your Work.**

Highlighting Your Work

- Have a place that showcases what's been accomplished.
- A location that will highlight the work you've done.
- This will allow for an increased level of credibility.

How To Set Up A Website

Taking time to establish your online presence with a website is key to having a successful business. It's necessary to set up a website and this lesson will show you step-by-step on how to make this happen with ease.

Step-By-Step Guide On Creating A Website

Step #1: **Setting Up A Website.**

> **1. Domain Name**
> **2. Hosting**
> **3. Website**

Three things necessary to set up a website:

- **Domain name**—A website name that's chosen and this is your online real estate.
- **Hosting**—Where *data* is stored from the website.
- **Website**—Actual place where you *build* the site.

Step #2: **Use Bluehost To Set Up.**

- Choose a ***plan*** that best suits individual needs and possibly upgrade later.
- Get a **free domain** name by signing up on the site.

Step #3: Set Up WordPress To Build A Website.

- Go to the website section and click install **WordPress**.
- Put in the *domain name* and click next.
- Enter the admin name and password and go to the WordPress site.
- Receive a link to access the admin dashboard.

Step #4: Go To WordPress Dashboard.

- WordPress Admin login.

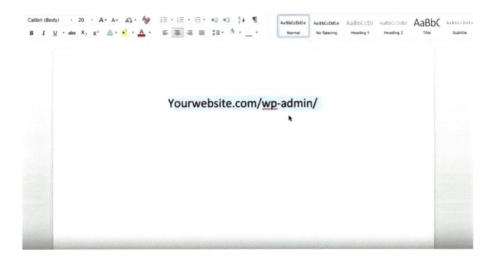

- WordPress dashboard is where *building* of the website actually begins.

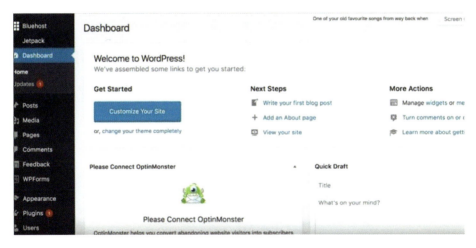

- Pick a *theme* and start building out the entire website.

5 Alternative Ways To Build A Website

WordPress is one of the most widely used platforms when it comes to creating a website. However, there are many alternative methods to help do so and this chapter will discuss five additional ways for building a website.

Different Methods For Creating A Website

Method #1: **Squarespace.**

- Drag and drop website builder.
- Comes with a monthly fee and easy for beginners.

Method #2: **Wix.**

- Many templates to choose from and this is a drag and drop type.
- There is a monthly fee.
- An alternative to WordPress.

Method #3: **Sitebuilder.com.**

- Offers a variety of different designs to meet your individual needs.
- Simple to use and requires payment of a monthly fee.

Method #4: **Outsourcing.**

Outsourcing

- Allows for more customization for a website.
- Hire a freelancer to do this for you.
- Much more expensive in most cases to complete.

Method #5: **Do-It-Yourself.**

- The least expensive method for creating a website.
- Takes a lot of time and effort to complete from scratch.

Tools For Websites

It's ideal to know the right tools to help optimize and customize your website. This lesson dives into the various top tools for creating a stellar site.

Top Tips When Creating A Website

Tip #1: **Website Themes.**

- Use *WordPress* to see all the themes that are being offered. This is accessible through the dashboard.
- *ThemeForest* is a website that offers a lot of themes when building a site.
- *Themifyme* offers a wide variety of **themes** from which to choose.

Tip #2: **Keep It Simple.**

- The best way to get your point across about any products or services being offered is by keeping your site simple and clean.
- Avoid putting too much on your site because this can over-complicate the message.
- Create a clean path for people and avoid being overwhelming to your viewers.

Tip #3: **Page Builders.**

Page builders are drag and drop tools that allow for building opt-in pages, sales pages and other pages necessary for a website.

Below are the top ones:

Page Builders

- **Instabuilder**—The least expensive for WordPress and it's only necessary to pay a one time fee. Very simple to use for building a site and allows for creating any type of page.
- **Optimizepress**—WordPress program that is a one time fee and has a feature that allows you to create a membership portal.
- **LeadPages**—It's necessary to pay per month and it's one of the easiest ones to use. Offers a very professional look.
- **ClickFunnels**—This offers every page you would ever need for any aspect of a website.

Clickfunnels is the most expensive and offers the most features including an email marketing service.

Keys To A Great Website

The first step in growing an online business is having a website that can allow you to do so. This lesson goes into detail about the keys to creating a great website.

Top Tips For Building A Site That Gets Attention

Tip #1: **Clarity.**

- It's necessary to be *clear* in what the website is all about or most **visitors** will leave.
- State what the business is and how *exactly* the products or services available can help others.

Tip #2: **Visually Appealing.**

- Ensure any website is *attractive* and offers the right amount of **appeal** to a visitor.
- Keep it *simple* and clean to look good.
- Be sure to *decrease* any clutter on the site.

Tip #3: **Easy To Navigate.**

- Must be *simple* to get around and fast for the user.
- The menus need to be **clear** for individuals or they may leave.

Easy To Navigate

Tip #4: **Mobile Friendly.**

- This is a world that is on the go and it's necessary to have a website that is easy to use on a mobile device.
- Select a theme that is mobile compatible and friendly.

Tip #5: **Directs People Towards A Specific Goal.**

- *Provide* instant information about what the website can offer others.
- Direct the users toward a **specific** goal and show the main point of the business.

Directs People Towards A Specific Goal

Tip #6: **Key Features.**

Having certain items on the website is ideal and below are features that should be offered:

- *Blogs*—Create a blog that offers a number of *informative* articles to people that visit the site. These can address **problems** and answer **questions** that can help drive traffic.
- *About page*—It's necessary to be **clear** telling others what your business is about and can help familiarize others with the brand.
- *Contact page*—Necessary to have a way for others to *contact* you and immediately know how to reach you.

- ***Email signup*** - It's crucial to ***build*** an email list to have the most successful and this can be done with a signup box.

Driving Traffic To Your Website

Traffic is the fuel that keeps your business running. It's critical to get viewers to your website. This lesson provides the best possible tools to do so and allows any site to rank higher on Google.

Top Tips For Getting More Customers

Tip #1: **Use Search Engine Optimization.**

- Rely on SEO strategies to allow for ranking higher on Google.
- Content is critical in using SEO because this is what is used to optimize a website. Should be

high-quality content that answers popular questions and addresses problems.
- Necessary to have specific keywords that individuals are using to search for an item.
- Links are the currency of the Internet and provides credibility. The more incoming links the higher the ranking may be.

Tip #2: **Social Media.**
- Relying on Facebook, Instagram, Twitter or other social media platforms to advertise your business and drive traffic.

- Necessary to post regularly to gain a following on social media and over time is the key to driving more traffic.
- Engage with others and create content that makes others want to ask questions and can start the communication ball rolling.
- Share links to your site on social media that allow others to resolve issues and enables people to visit your site.

Tip #3: **Create Ads.**

Best and easiest places to start placing ads:

- *Facebook*—The ideal place to begin your advertising and it's a huge platform. There are many people in every demographic. Regardless of the niche it's possible to target the individuals necessary to build a more successful company.
- *YouTube*—Great place for advertising because it's not as crowded as many of the other platforms. It requires a bit more learning but it's fairly inexpensive.
- *Influencer Marketing*—This involves using another individual's following or credibility as advertising. Paying to get your message in front of others that are following the influencers. More like a recommendation or word of mouth method of advertising.

Stats For Success

It's critical to monitor the stats of any website to determine how well it's being optimized. This chapter dives into various types of easy tools that any website owner can put to work immediately.

Steps For Ensuring A Website Gets Traffic

Step #1: **Use Easy Tools.**

Essential to keep track of the website stats to ensure a site is properly optimized.

Below are easy tools to use:

- **Google Analytics**—Easy to set up and necessary if you have a *website*. The best tool to learn the stats for any website.

- **PageSpeed Insights**—It's ideal to know how fast page loads on a website and this tool will show this. Provides a good idea of the user's experience while visiting the site.

- **SimilarWeb**—Allows a **website** owner to know what to look for when it comes to similar traffic. This tool answers questions, such as where is the **traffic** coming from, where it's going to and how much another website is getting and then apply this to your website.

Step #2: **What To Look For.**

- *Popular Pages*—Which pages of the **website** are visited the most frequently? This will allow you to see what is working to assist in getting **traffic**.

- *Time Spent-* The amount of time people spend on a **website**. It's possible to do this for individual pages and work to ensure it's compelling enough by providing good **content** up front.

- *Clicks-* Where are most individuals *clicking* on the website? It's ideal to know where and on what pages the most clicks are happening on a routine basis.

- *Traffic Sources*—Provides top traffic sources and enables you to see what works and what doesn't to determine if changes should be made or not.

Basic things like this will provide a greater overall perspective for any website. Use these steps to allow for significant improvement of the website.

A Giveaway

I have a very special gift for you!

We make smart and easy explainer content on a variety of different subjects. So, because you have shown interest in one of our products, we are giving away our bestselling courses (cost $20) absolutely FREE!

GOTO – **arxreads.com/gift** and grab yours now!

We hope you found this book helpful and if you did, we'd love for you to share your thoughts by leaving us a review of this book. If you have any questions you would like to ask you can reach out to us at *hi@arxreads.com* and we'll be sure to get back to you as soon as possible.

Thank you!

Printed in Great Britain
by Amazon